Tales of King Arthur

A Play

John Chambers

A SAMUEL FRENCH ACTING EDITION

FOUNDED 1830

SAMUELFRENCH-LONDON.CO.UK
SAMUELFRENCH.COM

Copyright © 1996 by John Chambers
All Rights Reserved

TALES OF KING ARTHUR is fully protected under the copyright laws of the British Commonwealth, including Canada, the United States of America, and all other countries of the Copyright Union. All rights, including professional and amateur stage productions, recitation, lecturing, public reading, motion picture, radio broadcasting, television and the rights of translation into foreign languages are strictly reserved.

ISBN 978-0-573-05110-4

www.samuelfrench-london.co.uk

www.samuelfrench.com

FOR AMATEUR PRODUCTION ENQUIRIES

UNITED KINGDOM AND WORLD EXCLUDING NORTH AMERICA

plays@SamuelFrench-London.co.uk

020 7255 4302/01

Each title is subject to availability from Samuel French, depending upon country of performance.

CAUTION: Professional and amateur producers are hereby warned that *TALES OF KING ARTHUR* is subject to a licensing fee. Publication of this play does not imply availability for performance. Both amateurs and professionals considering a production are strongly advised to apply to the appropriate agent before starting rehearsals, advertising, or booking a theatre. A licensing fee must be paid whether the title is presented for charity or gain and whether or not admission is charged.

The professional rights in this play are controlled by David Higham Associates Ltd, 7th Floor, Waverley House, 7–12 Noel Street, London W1F 8GQ.

No one shall make any changes in this title for the purpose of production. No part of this book may be reproduced, stored in a retrieval system, or transmitted in any form, by any means, now known or yet to be invented, including mechanical, electronic, photocopying, recording, videotaping, or otherwise, without the prior written permission of the publisher. No one shall upload this title, or part of this title, to any social media websites.

The right of John Chambers to be identified as author of this work has been asserted by him in accordance with Section 77 of the Copyright, Designs and Patents Act 1988

TALES OF KING ARTHUR

First produced on 7 June 1990, by the Dukes Playhouse, as a promenade production in Williamson Park, Lancaster, with the following cast:

Mordred	Julian Bleach
Bors	Ian Blower
Kay/King Pelles	Roger Delves-Broughton
Guinevere/Third Grail Maiden Second Demon	Barbara Dryhurst
Dindrane/Second Grail Maiden White Knight's Wife	Jacqueline Dutoit
Lancelot	Jim Findley
Percivale/First Monk	Peter Glancy
King Pellinore/White-Green Knight Knight of the Forest	Stephen Ley
Gawain	Nicholas Murchie
Morgana/Lady of the Lake	Siobhan Nicholas
Elaine/Lady of Blanchfleur First Grail Maiden/First Demon Woman with Baby	Kate Paul
Galahad/Red Knight/Messenger	Ian Poitier
Merlin (Sir Gonemans) Second Monk	Ted Richards
Arthur/Third Monk	Mark Spalding

Director **Ian Forrest**
Designer **Ashley Shairp**

The version printed here was adapted for Manchester Youth Theatre's production at the Forum Theatre, Manchester, directed by Noreen Kershaw, in September 1991.

CHARACTERS

Igrayne
Merlin (sometimes **Gonemans The Hermit**)
Kay
Arthur
Guinevere
Lancelot
Bors
Two Monks
Mordred
Morgana
Gawain
Creep the Messenger
King Pellinore
Lady of the Lake
Lady Blanchfleur (also Grail Maiden)
Percivale
Dindrane (also Grail Maiden)
Archbishop
Sir Ector
Two Ladies in Waiting
Red Knight
Green Knight (also White Knight)
Lady Catherine
Giles, a Squire
Elaine
Queen Pellesse
Armourer
Galahad
Abbess of the Pathway
Knight of the Forest
Dragon
Two Demons
Two Grail Maidens

Production Notes

The Lake and the Sword

The lake can be achieved by stretching a sheet of light fabric across the stage with the cast/stage management rippling it. The sword can be placed in a stylised way into the lake. (Throwing a sword on stage is strongly advised against, and would not achieve the best effect).

The Green Knight

The decapitation of the Green Knight is best achieved by the actor wearing bulky armour and helmet. The actor's head remains within the body of the armour, not the helmet!

John Chambers

ACT I

Scene 1

The mournful chants of monks hang over the trees like the mist. Far off, a woman screams

Igrayne (*off*) You cannot take my baby. You must not. You dare not. Oh please, do not take my son.

A hooded figure enters, hurrying, with a baby

Igrayne, also with a baby, tries to follow but is transfixed

Who would take a child from his mother? What cruel meaning is there to this madness? Queen I might be, but all the power I hold will not lessen my pain. (*She looks at the baby in her arms*) What wicked curse has been put on his half-sister? She smiles a wicked smile as you leave with my son. (*She sobs defeated*) Do not take my baby.

Igrayne exits, returning home defeated

Merlin appears, perhaps heralded by a spell which causes the mist to change colour

Merlin (*to the audience*) That was sixteen years ago—the boy child wasn't *stolen*, he was *rescued*. Rescued from a threat of evil which will continue to stalk him. Yes, sixteen years, gone in an instant. Time is as fragile as the mist over this enchanted place. It is not fixed. Fifteen centuries, separating you and I have been wafted away, as surely as will this mist. Dismissed by stories passed down by firesides. You will feel as our brave knights did—afraid that good will never triumph, wondering if your heart will stand the test of your quest. For *beware*—be ever alert, for things and people are not always what they might seem.

He is interrupted by the arrival of Kay, twenty, and his younger brother Arthur, sixteen

But time will not wait for us. Today the realm of Logres seeks a new king.

Merlin exits, unseen by Kay and Arthur

Kay walks in an exaggerated "manly" fashion. There is no sword in his scabbard, but he hasn't realized that. Arthur follows, imitating his walk. Kay suspects this, and occasionally looks behind, when Arthur instantly stops

Arthur Kay, tell me something.
Kay All right. (*He thinks*) I can tell you that little brothers are a nuisance.
Arthur (*persisting*) Why do you walk like that?
Kay Like what?
Arthur Like this. (*He does a grotesque imitation*)
Kay I don't. I walk like this. (*He does a walk just as bizarre, continuing*) I walk like this because I am approaching manhood. Because I will be one of the bravest knights in Logres. Because I will despatch villains, not just by the cut of my sword and the power of my lance. I will fill them with fear with my steely glint (*he leers*) and my manly gait. (*He swaggers*)
Arthur I suppose pulling a face like that might scare off some ne'er-do-wells. It'll probably stop the hens laying, too.
Kay How old are you, Arthur?
Arthur I'm sixteen.
Kay Well, don't expect to see seventeen.
Arthur Kay...
Kay What now?
Arthur You're going to need more than a squint and a strange walk to fight at the tournament.
Kay Of course, I will defeat all comers with my shining sharpened sword ... and be declared King of Logres. (*He goes to draw his sword—but it isn't in its scabbard*)
Arthur Is it invisible?
Kay It's your fault—you pestered me so much I forgot it. Run back home for it.
Arthur Three groats?
Kay One.
Arthur Two.
Kay Agreed. Now hurry.

Act I, Scene 1   3

Arthur (*holding out his hand*) Give me the money.
Kay I'll give you a kick up the backside—Now hurry.

Kay goes off

Arthur is about to run back

Guinevere enters

A moment between them

Guinevere You are Kay's brother, Arthur.
Arthur I am Arthur—I just happen to have a half-brother called Kay, who happens to have a mind like a sieve and walks as if someone has dropped a red hot horseshoe down his breeches.
Guinevere (*laughing*) My name is Guinevere, everyone calls me Guin.
Arthur I'll call you Guinevere.
Guinevere You think you are out of the ordinary.
Arthur I'm extraordinary.

Kay enters

Kay (*angrily*) I've a good mind to boil your head in goose fat. (*He sees Guinevere and bows grandly*) Lady Guinevere.
Arthur Everyone calls her Guin.
Kay Guin.
Arthur Well, ordinary people do.
Guinevere Isn't it exciting—the choosing of a new king.
Arthur How do they choose him?
Kay Any fool knows that—we all fight each other and when I've won, they crown me. Now bring me my sword. (*He stamps his foot*)

Arthur and Guinevere exchange a lingering look

Arthur leaves

Guinevere He's sweet.
Kay Sssh... He's got ideas above his station without a fair damsel such as you offering charitable flattery. (*He adopts his bold knight stance*) Methinks you need a bold brave fellow...

Lancelot and his cousin Bors enter

Whilst Kay waxes lyrical, Guinevere's attention is attracted by the arrival of the newcomers

> A man who will lead other men, a man who will be a knight ... and, who knows, perhaps a king.
>
> **Guinevere** (*absently*) You speak the truth, Kay.
> **Kay** (*proudly*) Yes. (*He sees who she's looking at*) Oh.

Lancelot and Bors call to them. They come from Gwynned

> **Lancelot** Boyo.
> **Kay** Who the devil does he think he's addressing?
> **Lancelot** Yes, you.
> **Guinevere** I think he's talking to you.
> **Bors** Could you help us, miss.
> **Guinevere** If I can.
> **Bors** I am Bors de Gannis and this is my cousin Lancelot of the Lake.
> **Lancelot** (*to Kay*) Could you feed our horses, lad. They're tethered in the wood.
> **Kay** What!
> **Lancelot** (*aside to Guinevere*) Is he hard of hearing as well as slow of mind?
> **Kay** I am Kay, son of Sir Ector. For your insults I *would* challenge you.

Lancelot draws his sword

> **Lancelot** Fine, a little sport. Some practice before the contest to choose a new king begins.
> **Kay** I say, I *would* challenge you—but as you see I am without sword. What a shame.
> **Guinevere** I'm sure Bors here would lend you his.

Bors offers his sword to the rapidly panicking Kay

> **Kay** Do you think I could fight with *that*! I wouldn't stir my gruel with that.

Lancelot raises his sword to Kay's throat

Act I, Scene 1

Lancelot You challenged me, sir.
Bors (*laughing suddenly*) He's got you beaten, Lancelot.
Lancelot How! He won't fight.
Bors He is greater than you——
Kay Listen to your cousin, sir.
Bors —he is a greater windbag, a greater show-off, and a greater idiot.

Guinevere laughs, then Lancelot, who lowers his sword

Guinevere Why have you come to Camelot?
Lancelot Lady Nimue, an enchantress in our homeland of Gwynedd——
Kay Ah, Welsh—that explains your impudence.
Bors (*to Kay*) What's your excuse?
Kay (*quietly*) If only I had my sword.
Lancelot —told us to find the wizard Merlin.
Kay That old bundle of twine and gristle.

Merlin enters, unseen by Kay

> That ancient bag of sinew and bones.
> That superstitious messenger of doom and gloom.
> That beard set on spindly legs.
> That magician without magic.

A gesture from Merlin and Kay loses the power of speech

Guinevere Merlin.
Merlin I greet you, Lancelot and Bors. Nimue ensured your safe passage from Gwynedd, I see.
Lancelot (*still amazed at Kay*) Yes.
Bors The Lady Nimue said that we must put our futures, our trust, in you.
Merlin I can point the way of your future, Bors, but you must have trust in yourselves, for you have great tasks to undertake, and there are evil forces set to make you fail. But the greatest threat to your success will be within yourselves—not just you, Lancelot and Bors, but others who will join you—to serve the new king.
Guinevere Who will be king?
Merlin Someone good, brave, and true. Someone who is close by at this moment.
Guinevere (*looking at Lancelot*) Yes, I think you are right.

Bors Merlin... (*He indicates Kay*) Is he struck dumb permanently?
Merlin Ah, I forgot. One's memory tends to fade at my age—seven hundred and forty-one years.

He releases Kay from the spell

Kay Merlin, o master. How good to see you. We were just talking about you. (*To the others*) Weren't we all? I was convincing our Celtic visitors that you really weren't the bag of old bones they believed you were. I was so pleased to see you I temporarily lost the power of speech. Nevertheless, I could still hear. And this business about the new king being near at hand. (*He struts his manly walk*) Need I say more.

All are amused

Merlin No, Kay, you need not.
Kay (*smugly*) I knew it. King Kay of Logres...
Merlin If the new king needs a jester, I will certainly, without hesitation, reservation, or prevarication, recommend you. Bundle of twine and bones indeed!

Mordred comes along with Morgana, disguised as an old crone, her features hidden by shawl and hair

Kay (*calling*) It's no good, Mordred—helping that old crone won't put you in the running for monarchy.
Guinevere Mordred is surely the slyest, most ambitious person in Logres.
Merlin There is one slyer, a person whose cunning ambition is only matched by her own wickedness.
Bors Who's that, then?
Merlin Morgana le Fay.

As Mordred and the crone pass the group, they stop. The crone mumbles incoherently, then, with a flourish, she waves her hand in their direction. She casts a spell, summoning up the powers of hell, and they are frozen. She discards the dreary robes to reveal herself, Morgana

Morgana (*circling the group*) See, Mordred—peasants under my absolute power. Nothing more than ridiculous statues, pathetic playthings.

Act I, Scene 1

Mordred With powers like that, Lady Morgana, you could install the new king. (*Hinting*) I'd see that you were looked after.

Morgana Do not scheme and connive with me, Mordred. Power will be yours when *I* am ready. I do not *need* anyone... But of course, I will reward those who serve me well.

Mordred kisses her hand. Merlin starts to move, breaking away from the spell

Mordred Madam, the wizard—he moves. Use your superior powers to defeat, destroy him.

Morgana is now worried. Merlin turns slowly, but does not yet face her. As Morgana holds her hand towards Merlin, trying to strengthen her spell, she shakes and quivers as his powers assert themselves

Kill them!
Morgana Do not imply that I could not.
Mordred I don't.
Morgana I could kill you now in an instant.
Mordred Why don't you kill them?
Morgana I need them. For there is something sacred, something holy and pure—that only the future king and a handful of his followers can find. The stars predict this. They must find it, lead me to it. Then by all that is unholy I will destroy this object and Logres will then ever be subservient to me. (*One final flourish to hold her spell. To the audience*) Be warned—I will ever be near. In the brightest sunshine and in the shadows of the darkest glen and valley, a cold shiver will tell you I am near.

Morgana leaves

Merlin first, then the others, are released from their spell. For all but Merlin it is as if nothing has happened

Lancelot So good wizard, how and when will the new king be chosen? It must be the grandest of tournaments.

Merlin goes to Morgana's discarded robe

Merlin (*to Mordred*) Where is the crone?
Mordred (*lying*) Gone to feed her pigs, I dare say.
Merlin Gone to lay plans for an age of cruel darkness would be nearer the truth. (*To the others*) Come, you ask when and how the new king will be chosen. The answer is now, and this is how.
Guinevere So soon?
Merlin There is evil abroad. No time can be lost. Messengers have travelled the length and breadth of the realm. Come now, good men brave. The test of the sword shall point out the new King of Logres.
Bors (*to Lancelot*) If it's a test of goodness, bravery and the sword, by sunset you'll be king.
Lancelot And what a fair queen Guinevere would make.

Merlin leads them to a place where he will find the sword in the stone

Other men enter. Gawain is one of the group of bystanders

Merlin reveals the stone with the sword

Merlin He who pulls this sword from the stone will be king.
Kay (*aside*) A relief I have to say—I stand a better chance tussling with the sword in the stone than if it was in the hand of Lancelot of the Lake.

Merlin and Guinevere stand by the stone

Morgana appears some distance away, watching unseen

The men queue—first Kay, bustling to the front, then Mordred, Bors, Gawain, and Lancelot, and then any others who might try

(*Loudly*) Do not waste your precious time waiting and hoping. Practise bowing if you want to gainfully occupy yourselves.
Mordred Get on with it, you pompous windbag.
Kay Don't expect to be mentioned in my birthday honours list, Mordred.

Kay tries desperately but cannot move the sword

Merlin It is not to be—the sword will slide as surely as if it were greased in a loose scabbard—*if* he who pulls is heir to the throne.
Kay (*grumbling, to the others*) I've loosened it for you.

Act I, Scene 1

Mordred steps up

Merlin Mordred—draw the sword if you can.

Morgana, unseen by the others, matches Mordred's movements and calls her encouragement

Morgana Come, Mordred, pull, with my power it will be a simple matter and then my agent will be enthroned.

After much effort, Mordred lets go of the sword with a yell, his hands burning. Morgana matches his action

Mordred What sorcery, magician?
Merlin No sorcery, Mordred—the blade measures bravery and goodness. I don't doubt your bravery, but...
Mordred (*to the others*) Are we to base the rule of Logres on a fairground magic trick?
Kay No, why don't we give it to the poorest loser, the biggest sulker...

The others laugh at Mordred

Merlin (*to Gawain*) And you, young sir.
Gawain I am Gawain.
Merlin This is a name I believe we will hear many times in years to come.
Guinevere Is this young man to be our new king?

Gawain pulls the sword but fails

Gawain Not I, Lady Guinevere.
Merlin You, Bors.
Bors I don't think there's a lot of point my trying—stronger, braver and more goodly men have tried.
Guinevere You must, Bors—Logres would not want for a more gentle sovereign if you succeeded.
Lancelot Go on, cousin.
Kay Gentle! Bor by name, bore by nature.

Bors attempts the sword, not as fiercely determined as the others, and good-natured when he fails

Bors Now you, Lancelot.
Lancelot (*to Guinevere as he is about to try*) Would you marry the King of Logres?
Guinevere And become Queen?
Lancelot I can think of no-one better.
Guinevere If the King were to ask me, I would pledge now, on my life, that I would, *will*, marry him.
Bors There's an incentive, Lancelot.
Merlin Guinevere will become Queen.

She and Lancelot share a moment. He confidently pulls the sword but it will not move

Lancelot What tricks are you playing, Merlin?
Merlin No tricks, Lancelot. You will become one of the greatest knights Logres will ever see.
Guinevere But not king.
Mordred Who the devil will be king?
Merlin Time will tell.

Others try but with no success. They move away from the sword in the stone. Morgana watches this

Morgana Fools. Logres will drift, without someone at the helm. Drift towards the deadly maelstrom which I will cause.

Arthur enters, still without Kay's sword

No-one apart from Morgana sees him

Arthur (*grumbling*) If Kay thinks I am going all the way back for his sword, he's got another thought coming. (*He notices the sword in the stone*) Here's a bit of luck. (*He looks about*) Stupid place to leave a sword. (*He walks to the sword; without fuss, he draws it from the stone*)

There is music

Morgana (*screaming*) No, not him. Not him.

Morgana exits

Act I, Scene 1

The others turn and see Arthur with the sword

Merlin Our King has come.
Kay Arthur? Arthur!

Lancelot and Bors go down on one knee. The others follow their example. Mordred reluctantly last

    (*Whispering to Arthur*) I didn't really mean you were a nuisance.
Arthur Oh... I see ... a joke at my expense.
Mordred At *our* expense.
Merlin This is no joke, Arthur, son of King Uther Pendragon.
Arthur King Uther? King Ector is my father.
Merlin King Ector took you in when I rescued you as a baby.
Arthur From who?
Merlin Evil forces were out to stop you becoming King.
Arthur Who?
Merlin You will discover that soon enough—but first you must be crowned.
Guinevere I will not *serve* our chosen King.

They look at her

    I made a pledge. If he would ask I will not be his *servant*—but his wife.
Arthur Will you be my queen?
Guinevere (*glancing at Lancelot*) I have made a pledge, (*to Arthur*) I will be your queen.
Bors (*raising his sword*) Long live the King.
Lancelot Long live the King and Queen.

Creep, the messenger, enters, interrupting the celebrations, and approaches Merlin. Creep has a strange "creeping" walk

Kay Who goes there?
Creep Creep's the name, message abringing's my game.
Merlin What news?
Creep Before I say anything, I want to know if you have that rotten custom the Romans have? You know—the one where they (*he makes a throat-slitting action*) if the poor soul brings bad news?

Arthur Of course not.
Creep (*relieved*) Oh, I'll tell you then. My guv'nor, King Pellinore—as crazy a cove as ever sat astride a stallion, says he will be king, and he's sworn to (*he makes a throat-slitting action*) anyone as says different, 'e do.
Lancelot We will soon sort him out.

Gawain and Bors are immediately ready to go to meet the challenge

Arthur Wait.
Kay Let them go. This Pellinore insults us all.
Arthur I know—and because of that, I must go. I am a king by chance——
Kay All kings are.
Arthur —but I must *earn* my right, *prove* myself.
Bors Let us come.
Arthur No, Bors. You must all go to Camelot—prepare for a grand coronation *and* wedding. Merlin can accompany me.
Kay What use is he in a fight—if a fly lands on his shoulder he nearly topples over.
Arthur He can instruct me in my duties. They didn't teach me how to be a king at school. Come, Merlin. (*As he goes*) I will see you all soon.

Guinevere runs to him

Guinevere Take care, Arthur.

They kiss lightly

Arthur Lancelot—take care of Guinevere.

Lancelot hesitates

I can think of no-one she would be safer with.
Merlin (*to Creep*) Now, lead us to your master.
Creep Walk this way.

Creep goes off

Arthur and Merlin shrug and walk as Creep does. They exit

Act I, Scene 2

Lancelot, Guinevere and then the others leave for Camelot

SCENE 2

By the lake of Avalon

Mists, and angels singing

Arthur waits

King Pellinore, in full armour, appears. Creep is with him

Creep He's here, sire, he's here. I told you I'd brung him.
Pellinore What do you want?
Arthur To pass this way.
Pellinore Who are you?
Arthur My name's Arthur Pendragon.
Pellinore Of course you can pass this way ... but you must kill me first.
Arthur Thank you.
Pellinore Why do you thank me?
Arthur Because I've been looking for a challenge, a quest. And to defeat a tyrant such as you, Pellinore, will fit the bill nicely.
Pellinore Yes, I am King Pellinore, sonny, and I've seen off a lot stronger men than you.

Merlin hurries on to the scene

Merlin (*to Arthur*) My Lord, wait. Take another route. Don't fight him. You are of no use to the people of Logres dead.
Creep (*to the audience*) All the same, these noblemen—I mean, anyone with an ounce of sense would go another way round—but do they listen?
Arthur I need a challenge to prove I'm a worthy monarch. I can't think of a better one than (*louder for Pellinore's benefit*) that so-called King ... more of a bully, I'd say.

Pellinore comes charging at Arthur, lance lowered. Merlin gets out of the way

Merlin (*hurrying*) Oh dear, I think some bones are going to be crunched, some blood splattered.

Arthur skilfully knocks the lance out of Pellinore's hand. Pellinore takes his sword from its scabbard

Pellinore You're brave, Arthur Pendragon——
Arthur And you're a coward.
Pellinore —and you're a fool. (*He charges again. With one blow, he breaks Arthur's sword. He puts his sword to Arthur's throat*)

Merlin hurries to them

Yield or die.
Merlin Wait!
Pellinore I'll skewer you on the same sword, old man.
Merlin Oh dear, oh dear, oh dear.
Arthur I would rather die than yield.
Pellinore (*raising his sword to strike Arthur*) Your wish is granted.
Merlin (*touching Pellinore's shoulder*) Stay! This is King Arthur. If you kill him, Logres will face an age of darkness.
Pellinore (*hesitating*) If I spare him, he will not forgive me for attacking him when he was barely armed.
Merlin (*raising a hand before Pellinore's face*) He will forgive you and in times to come you will be an ally to Arthur. Now, go.

A moment, then Pellinore turns, as if in a trance, and goes to leave. Creep scurries after him

Creep Wake up, guv'nor ... on seconds thoughts, don't. You won't bully and boss me in that condition.

Pellinore and Creep exit

Arthur What have you done to him, what magic?
Merlin It doesn't matter. What matters is that you are less headstrong. The good of your kingdom is more important than your pride.
Arthur I'm a fine king. Defeated, and without even a sword. (*He indicates the broken hilt*)
Merlin Wait here by the Lake of Avalon and you might find a new sword. Becoming a fine king might take a little longer.

Merlin leaves

Act I, Scene 2

Arthur paces about, looking for a sword

Arthur I see no sword.

Haunting heavenly singing fills the air

Across the lake, a woman appears: it is the Lady of the Lake. She walks over the water towards Arthur

Who are you?
Lady of the Lake I am the Lady of the Lake. Why do you wait here?
Arthur The good wizard Merlin says that I will find a sword here. But I can't find one.
Lady of the Lake You will have your sword, King Arthur.
Arthur How do you know me?
Lady of the Lake The Lake will provide the sword you seek. It will be called Excalibur. Wear its scabbard always and it will protect you—for it is magic, made by the fairies of Avalon.

Arthur watches the lake

The Lady, unseen by Arthur, leaves

The Lights change, the scene becomes more magical. From the lake, an arm appears, holding aloft Excalibur in its sheath. He takes the sword. The arm returns to the water and Arthur goes to the shore and examines the sword. He turns to thank the Lady, but then realizes she has gone

Arthur Thank... Thank you, mysterious Lady of the Lake wherever you are. (*He brandishes Excalibur*) Holding this sword I feel its power well through my body. I feel now, like a king. Now for Camelot. Wait until I tell Guinevere. It will make her proud that, I, Arthur, will be her King.

Arthur leaves

Lady Blanchfleur enters. She looks in the direction Arthur has gone, having seen what happened

Blanchfleur This place is truly magical. I have seen a boy king take his enchanted sword from the waters of the lake. But where is my magic destiny? Inside I *feel* that fate has a great purpose for me... (*Wryly*) But you delude yourself, Blanchfleur. There is no greet purpose. Apart from resting by the Lake and dreaming. That is the most you can expect. (*She falls asleep. Murmurs*) Sweet, sweet dreams.

Percivale, poorly dressed, carrying a roughly-hewn spear, and his sister Dindrane, dressed simply, almost nun-like, appear. They do not yet see Blanchfleur

Percivale Be honest, Dindrane, you think I'm a complete crackpot—to imagine that I could be a knight.
Dindrane It doesn't matter what I think, Percivale. If you believe it's right for you, then you should do all you can to achieve it.
Percivale You might be my little sister but you have more wisdom than a thousand scholars.
Dindrane (*smiling*) A thousand scholars! Don't be silly—nine hundred and ninety nine maybe!
Percivale (*laughing*) Come on then. Let's get to Camelot and see if this new king—what's his name—Albert?
Dindrane Arthur!
Percivale Let's see if he has a vacancy for a "knight". (*He looks down at his appearance*)
Dindrane A knight with the sharpest pointed stick in Logres.

As they are about to set off, Percivale sees the sleeping Blanchfleur

Percivale I wonder who she is.
Dindrane Let her sleep in peace.
Percivale (*admiring Blanchfleur*) Is it possible to fall in love with a face?
Dindrane No more than it is to fall in love with a mask.
Percivale I want to wake her, get to know her.
Dindrane How can you hope to be a knight if you are distracted by the first pretty face you see.
Percivale Why do you have to be so reasonable, so rational—so blessed right. (*He hesitates*) I know. (*He loosens his ring, takes Blanchfleur's, and exchanges it for his own*)
Dindrane What are you doing?
Percivale Swapping rings—she will wear my ring.

Act I, Scene 3   17

Dindrane Hers is valuable—a cluster of precious stones.
Percivale Mine is the only thing of any value I own—so it is of far greater value than hers. (*He kisses Blanchfleur on the cheek*) Sleep sweetly, my lady. My thoughts will be closer to you than my ring—until we meet again. I know we will... Farewell. (*He turns to Dindrane*) Come on, Dindrane, don't dawdle.

She smiles

Dindrane Camelot?
Percivale Camelot.

Percivale and Dindrane exit

Blanchfleur awakes, half aware that something has happened. She touches the ring, hesitates

Blanchfleur Perhaps my dreams and destiny are linked to another's.

Then she leaves in the opposite direction to Percivale

SCENE 3

Camelot. The Court of King Arthur. The Round Table

There can be juggling, sword fighting, singing. A sense of celebration

Kay bustles about, charged with organising the invitations. Percivale and Dindrane enter a little nervously

Kay (*bustling*) Come on. Get moving. This is to be a coronation and royal wedding, not a cattle market. (*To Percivale*) Are you the jester?
Percivale No, sir.
Kay You aren't an official guest.
Dindrane This is my brother Percivale. He has come to the Court of Camelot to offer his services as knight to the new king.
Kay Oh, how very gracious. We will all be able to sleep safe in our beds knowing a swineherd, whose sister speaks for him, is going to protect us.

Percivale I'm a *goat*herd.
Kay You're a nuisance.
Dindrane He's ten times the man you will ever be inspite of your finery.

Kay goes to strike her. Percivale steps forward and threatens Kay with his spear, but Dindrane stays his hand

Kay I am Sir Kay, the new king's brother.
Dindrane You should be better mannered, then.

Percivale and Kay square up. This is broken by a roar of drums

   Merlin enters

Merlin Lords, Ladies, people of Logres—your King and Queen.

Arthur, Guinevere; followed by Lancelot and Bors (who carry crowns), Gawain, and Mordred enter. Guinevere is attended by two ladies in waiting. Morgana lurks in the background, near Mordred

Arthur and Guinevere go to their thrones. We see the five empty sieges (chairs) which none will yet sit in and which are draped in silk (concealing the name of the future occupant). The central siege is slightly grander. The knights do not wear their helmets

   Sir Ector and the Archbishop enter

Archbishop Arthur, son of King Uther Pendragon and Queen Igrayne, by the will of the sword and the will of the people, you are King of the Realm of Logres.

Bors crowns Arthur

Merlin Guinevere, daughter of King Leodegraunce and Queen Elenore, by the will of the King and the will of the people, you are Queen of the Realm of Logres.

Lancelot takes Guinevere's crown and hesitates before placing it on her head

Act I, Scene 3   19

Morgana (*quietly to Mordred*) The seeds of destruction are sown even now. Lancelot and Guinevere can scarcely conceal their lust. And soon more splinters will be chiselled from the base of the throne.

Lancelot places the crown on Guinevere's head

Archbishop Long live the King and Queen.
Others Long live the King and Queen.
Arthur And now my first duty—to gather the knights who will sit at this Round Table.
Guinevere Why a round table?
Arthur Merlin?
Merlin So that no man can say he is higher or lower than another.
Arthur Sir Ector, my good foster father, I'd be honoured if you would read the names.
Sir Ector The first, sire.
Kay (*aside*) Sire! I still want to call him "nuisance"... (*He reads over Ector's shoulder*) The first on your list will be the bravest, most gallant you could ever wish to have at your side...
Guinevere It is Lancelot.
Kay It is me—Kay.

Kay kneels and Arthur dubs him

Arthur Arise, Sir Kay. (*Aside*) And be less big-headed in future.
Sir Ector (*reading*) Mordred.
Kay (*reading the list*) Mordred! (*Aside*) Mordred. That schemer Mordred.
Arthur (*aside*) Better he is where I can keep an eye on him.
Kay (*aside*) You'll need eyes in the back of your head. (*He smiles to Mordred*) Well done.
Morgana (*still unseen by others*) My agent Mordred is installed at the heart of things. The fool Arthur makes my task easier.

Arthur dubs Mordred

Arthur Arise, Sir Mordred.
Sir Ector (*reading*) Sir Bors.
Kay Bore.
Arthur Bor*s*.

Kay Ah, yes.

Bors comes forward and kneels

Arthur Bors—a knight of high virtue and great goodness. Arise, Sir Bors de Gannis. (*To Sir Ector*) I know who is next—Lancelot, one whose reputation reassures me that I can put my absolute trust in him.

Lancelot kneels

Arise, Sir Lancelot of the Lake. Be ever by my side.

Lancelot stands by Guinevere

Morgana See whose side he stands by.
Sir Ector And now Gawain, son of King Lot of Orkney.

Gawain kneels and Arthur dubs him

Arthur Arise, Sir Gawain. And now all of you who are to be Knights of the Round Table must accept The Orders of Chivalry and swear to keep them.
Sir Ector (*reading from a scroll*) All of you who sit at this table, and those who follow you in the future, are the Knights of Logres. You shall live in the Realm of Righteousness and the Glory of Logres. Do not ever depart from the high virtues of this Realm. Do not commit any cruel or wicked deed. Do not be either untruthful or engage in dishonest dealing. Be merciful. Do all in your power to comfort the sick and protect the weak. Do not use your authority or power for personal gain. Be just and righteous.
Arthur Let this be an example to all—for now and forever.
All Knights We so pledge to do.

Dindrane steps forward

Dindrane Why are all these knight of noble birth? It isn't any guarantee of their character.
Mordred And what would you know?
Dindrane I know a lot by looking at you.

Act I, Scene 3

Kay I suppose the sheep keeper would make a better knight.
Dindrane Don't dismiss Percivale because his hands are rough with labour and he hasn't rich parents to provide gawdy silks.
Percivale Hush Dindrane.
Arthur Let her speak for you, Percivale—no-one else at the Court will.
Dindrane I have spoken.
Kay So, everyone who has a sister to speak up for them should be made a knight?
Percivale Everyone should have the chance to prove themselves.

Kay laughs

Arthur I think what you say is fair, Percivale.
Merlin Wisely spoken.
Arthur (*picking up a goblet*) A toast to Percivale—for his cheek... But how might he prove himself...?

There is a sudden disturbance and the Red Knight enters

All are taken aback

Red Knight So, we have a new king. Ha. A witless boy and a clutch of jumped up squires who have ambitions above their station.

The knights draw their swords but the Red Knight is already by the King and Queen brandishing his sword

Frozen, are we? Rooted to the spot? Transfixed. Move a hair and your new Queen never will. (*He takes Arthur's goblet and drinks from it*) When I return, I will not only take your wine—your kingdom will be mine.

In a flourish, the Red Knight exits, taking the goblet

Lancelot Let's go and run him through.
Percivale (*shouting*) Sire—let me prove myself. If all your knights go, Camelot will be defenceless. Let me (*pointedly*) a humble goatherd go—without armour or sword.
Arthur Brave words.

Percivale I will return with your goblet and that rogue's armour for my own.

Arthur You have your wish granted. If you fail, return to the mountains and your sheep, not here. If you bring back my goblet, you will be made a knight.

Kay I fear you will not see the goblet again, brother.

Mordred (*impatiently*) Can we take our places at the Round Table now?

Merlin Yes, there is no reason why not.

Kay and Mordred each immediately head for a siege

Kay Nice of you to provide a grand throne for me, Merlin.

Mordred And this will suit me fine.

Merlin If either of you sit in those sieges your backsides will scorch and your mouths become as chimneys!

Kay Ha!

Merlin Try it.

Kay (*hesitating*) Who are the five sieges intended for?

Merlin (*removing the first cover slowly*) The five greatest knights this land will ever see. The five who will see the Grail. (*He removes the first cover to reveal Gawain's name*) Sir Gawain. (*He removes the next cover*) Sir Bors. (*He removes the next cover*) Sir Lancelot.

They take their seats

Mordred What about the other two?

Merlin All will be revealed in time. But I can tell you that he who will occupy this (*the grandest*) siege—The Siege Perilous, will be the greatest of all knights, and he is not yet born.

Proceedings are rudely interrupted by the arrival of a large and grotesque visitor, the Green Knight

Green Knight Much talk of bravery here. Much talk. Much talk. All talk. Much prattle about challenges and quests. Well, young King, here's a challenge, a quest which will not disrupt your present entertainments too much.

Arthur Who are you, Sir Knight?

Green Knight I am the Green Knight.

Act I, Scene 3

Kay I wouldn't like to hazard a guess why.
Green Knight My challenge is this: I will allow one of you a free blow at me. If I die, I die——
Kay A free blow? I'll do it.
Green Knight ——But if I live, I must return that blow after one year and one day.
Kay (*having doubts*) Mm... On second thoughts my services might be too valuable to lose. My little brother might not be able to cope without me. You try Mordred.
Morgana (*to Mordred*) Your head is more valuable to me on your shoulders.
Mordred I would not deign to belittle my knightly status by accepting a challenge from a talking tree.
Gawain (*coming forward*) I am Sir Gawain, and I accept your challenge, Green Knight. One blow?
Green Knight One blow.

Gawain draws his sword, hesitates

Come, on Gawain, hurry, man—old age will get me before your sword.

Gawain takes an almighty swing at the Green Knight's helmet—decapitating him in a moment. The knight sways, but remains standing. Gawain turns away satisfied—suddenly he freezes as the Green Knight speaks

I will see you in one year and one day, Gawain. Keep your neck well shaved.

Green Knight roars with laughter, picks up his own head, and leaves

Mordred (*aside to Morgana*) Gawain's siege might be vacant in one year and a day.
Morgana One by one, the Knights face their destiny, in each case almost certain death.
Lancelot We cannot sit here and allow every upstart to insult the throne. If the dark days of Logres are to be put behind us, we must seek out evil, not wait for it to call on us. With your permission, Lord, I will take my leave and go on such a quest.
Bors And I.

Guinevere Why must you leave, Lancelot? (*Quickly*) I mean, who will protect the Court?
Arthur I have Excalibur. Come, ready yourselves for the challenge ahead. (*He calls*) Armourer.

The Armourer enters

Sir Bors stands. Ladies-in-waiting will bring armour to Armourer who will assist dressing Bors

Bors I stand before you. Simply Bors, the man. An ordinary bloke.

Armourer brings a breast plate and fits it

Armourer A breast plate—that dazzles your enemies in the sun.
Bors And fries me like a strip of bacon on the inside.

Gauntlets are brought

Armourer Gauntlets to throw down a challenge, and withstand stray blades.
Bors To take the gentleness from my hands.

A helmet is brought

Armourer Your helmet to withstand blows and arrows if they glance it. (*He puts the helmet on, but the visor remains up*)

A lance is brought

Your lance, your spear. To joust with in sport, or to kill any who stand in your way. To make them keep their distance.
Bors I'm just an ordinary bloke.

A shield is brought

Armourer Your shield—to fend off attacks. To proclaim who you are by its crest. Any stranger, seeing the shield, knows who you are.
Bors But they don't know anything about me at all.

Act I, Scene 3   25

Armourer Your visor. To protect your face. To make a mask.
Bors To cover my fear. To hide the fact that I'm just an ordinary bloke.

Armourer slams down the visor. The transformation is complete

Lancelot goes to Guinevere whilst the other knights ready themselves. The two ladies-in-waiting turn away, obviously aware of their relationship

Lancelot Are you cross with me?
Guinevere No.
Lancelot I have my duties.
Guinevere Yes. Yes. I know.
Lancelot I'll miss you.
Guinevere I'll miss you.
Lancelot (*quickly*) As a knight would miss the Queen he would happily stay near to guard.
Guinevere Of course. Where will you go?
Lancelot To the Wastelands, to see if I can find the legendary Castle Carbonek.
Guinevere It is said to change form, and move its location; the scene of terrible events.
Lancelot Such a challenge might just occupy my thoughts so that I don't spend all my time thinking about——
Kay (*shouting*) Knights of the Round Table—prepare to leave.
Arthur May God go with you all as you begin your quest to banish the dark clouds, so that the sunlight of goodness shines once more on this fair kingdom. (*He sits on his throne, deep in thought*)

Gawain, Bors, and Lancelot (after a last wave to Guinevere) leave, all in different directions

Percivale bids farewell to Dindrane and he too goes

Dindrane is sad. Guinevere goes to her. Morgana and Mordred listen to their exchange

Guinevere (*taking her arm*) It is not easy to see a loved one leave, knowing you might never see him again.
Dindrane I believe you speak from experience, your Highness.

Morgana listens to the following

Guinevere You seem so naive——
Dindrane My background was humble, my experience limited.
Guinevere —but so knowing. As if you can see into my soul.
Dindrane I have no special powers.
Guinevere Do you see things in me that you despise, do you think I'm ambitious or disloyal?
Dindrane I hope I've not given you reasons to feel that.
Guinevere I feel an unease.
Dindrane I'll leave court if my presence disturbs you in any way.
Guinevere No, Dindrane, stay. I think it is my own presence that disturbs me. Be a lady-in-waiting.
Dindrane (*ironically*) We are both ladies-in-waiting—waiting, not doing.
Guinevere (*agreeing*) I believe I trust you. I'm a queen and I need a friend more so because of it. The men expect me to flatter, or concern myself with harmless, thoughtless activity—and many women would turn a given confidence from me into a spiteful weapon to use against me.

They leave

Morgana (*sarcastically*) Who on earth would want to do anything to hurt or harm our fair Queen.
Mordred Are you anything more than a gossip, Morgana?
Morgana I am not insulted by that, Mordred—because insults from an *idiot* have no value. But I will explain—every single action I take will have a single objective: For me, and those I choose, to rule this land. By *not* acting on occasions—it is not inertia, not sloth, not fear, it is because things are going my way. Because Arthur and his followers are flawed, and if they cause the downfall of this realm, who am I to stop them? (*She moves off a little distance*)

Mordred hesitates

Mordred (*aside*) I know she despises me. But this *"idiot"* knows when to be idiotic, not to be taken seriously. This idiot also knows when to act and when not to. This idiot will bide his time, wait for his moment. This realm will one day be ruled by an idiot. It will be my very own idiotic kingdom. (*He laughs*) Very good, Mordred ... the wittiest chap I know. (*He makes for the exit, pleased with himself*)

Arthur (*to Mordred*) Mordred, who is the lady you have been talking to?

Morgana hears this

Mordred (*evasively*) Which lady?
Morgana (*boldly*) I am Lady Morgana le Fay, sire.

Mordred exits

Arthur I seem to know you.
Morgana You have many subjects.
Arthur Have we ever met?
Morgana I do not think so.
Arthur Perhaps I dreamt I'd met you.
Morgana I'm very flattered.

Morgana curtsies and moves off

Merlin goes over to Arthur

Arthur I'm sure I've met the Lady Morgana.
Merlin You have.
Arthur When?
Merlin I cannot say.
Arthur Why?
Merlin When your mind is ready for you to remember, then you'll remember.
Arthur Why can't you give a straight answer?
Merlin Because it is better you distance yourself from her.
Arthur Does she wish me harm?
Merlin As long as you have Excalibur you will come to no harm—but you are a king, you possess power. For many that is worth more than any material wealth.
Arthur Does Morgana want my power?
Merlin Many people do. But let us not speculate on her. Today is your day.

Arthur and Merlin are alone

Arthur Merlin.

Merlin looks

A question.

Merlin nods

This might sound rather stupid.
Merlin A king can ask anything of anyone.
Arthur Right. What do kings do?
Merlin Ah, that one.
Arthur My Knights fight my battles for me. You advise me. I don't even have to open doors for myself. I can have everything I want, as much of it as I want. (*He pauses*) Is that why kings invade other lands. To make life interesting, to take things that aren't handed to them on a plate?
Merlin Yes, it probably is.
Arthur You must think I'm very foolish. You go to all this trouble to make me King, and I don't know what to make of it all.
Merlin Perhaps you are a king because you ask questions. Because you want to see reason.
Arthur But do people *need* a king?
Merlin Probably not.
Arthur That's what I thought.
Merlin But if they *think* they do, well, someone best do it.
Arthur Aren't I a fraud?
Merlin Not if your subjects believe in you with all their hearts. Not if you are as loyal to them. (*Beat*) What kind of kingdom do you want to rule?
Arthur A just kingdom. Where my knights protect the weak. Where we are honest, loyal. Where people can go about their business unmolested.
Merlin The oaths which your knights have taken are devised just to bring that about.
Arthur I hope so... But am I worthy?
Merlin Only you can decide that—and the way your subjects conduct themselves. The adventures your knights embark upon will be a test of you as much as of them.
Arthur I hope I do not fail them.

They walk slowly off

Act I, Scene 4   29

                                    SCENE 4

*A pavilion which, by changing the colour of the standard, will serve for
other encounters. Now it is the pavilion of the White Knight*

Gawain enters; he is anxious

Giles, the White Knight's squire, emerges from the pavilion

Giles What d'you want?
Gawain I seek the Green Knight.
Giles You must be crackers—as crazy as someone who's not a full ducket, I'd say.
Gawain In three days I have a meeting with him—he is sworn to revenge a blow I struck to his neck. What shall I do?
Giles Walk around like this. (*He hunches his head into his shoulders, and walks about in exaggerated fashion*)

The White Knight and Catherine, his wife, emerge from the pavilion

Catherine Who is our visitor, Giles?
Giles Someone who you better get to know pretty quickly if you want to get to know him at all.
Gawain I am Sir Gawain.
White Knight I am the White Knight, and this is my wife, Lady Catherine.
Catherine Husband, this young knight seems to bear the world's troubles on his shoulders.
Giles (*aside*) That's all he'll bear on his shoulders.
White Knight What troubles you, sir?
Gawain (*with bravado*) Troubles me! Nothing troubles me. Nothing dare trouble me—I am privileged to sit in a siege at the court of King Arthur.
White Knight It is good that you do not have a burden to carry.
Gawain Yes.
Catherine You have a naturally troubled brow, Sir Gawain?
Gawain (*irritably*) You, Sir White Knight, would be nervous, apprehensive, anxious if you had an appointment with a headless green giant. If you had to allow him a free blow on your neck with a sword. You would be a little ... a little...

White Knight I would be more than a little anything. I would be terrified, petrified, mortified, horrified. I would be so afraid that I might lose control over my bodily functions. (*He laughs*)
Gawain (*smiling*) Am I not entitled to furrow my brow?
Catherine Furrow it at your will.
White Knight And while you do, why not rest here. Carrying the world's burdens has clearly tired you.
Gawain I have to find the Green Knight.
White Knight He lives by the Green Chapel. I will direct you there. But first you must share our hospitality. Mustn't he?
Catherine Of course you must, Sir Gawain. Even if this is your last journey, as you say it might be—all the more reason to enjoy it.
Gawain (*not convinced*) It would be unchivalrous to refuse your hospitality.
White Knight Quite so. Now I must go hunting. Rest here, Sir Gawain, before you have your head shaved by this green monster. Lady Catherine will care for you.
Gawain That is very kind of you, sir.
White Knight But promise that no matter what temptation befalls you here, you will not abuse my trust.
Gawain You have my word as a Knight of Logres.

The White Knight leaves with Giles

Catherine gives Gawain a goblet of wine

(*Drinking*) Sweet, sweet wine. Its taste makes the leaving of life all the more bitter. I should be proud, euphoric. Going to die the death of a knight. What greater more fitting way is there for me to go. Keeping my promise to die at the hands of the great green monster.
Catherine But you don't feel proud? Euphoric?
Gawain I feel wretched. Trapped. And because of that, I feel guilty.
Catherine (*seductively*) But you have life now. What use are those silly vows and promises. They have no meaning. Kiss me. Compare that feeling to those your knightly quest engenders.
Gawain I promised your husband not to give in to any temptation. How can I betray his hospitality?
Catherine (*more ardently*) Dear Sir Gawain. Brave Sir Gawain. Young Sir Gawain. Handsome Sir Gawain. Many weeks you must have travelled without seeing a damsel such as I.

Act I, Scene 4

Gawain (*pretending this isn't happening*) Well, I think it's time I went off to seek out the old Green Knight.
Catherine You prefer him to me, sir?
Gawain (*aside*) Oh Merlin, where are you—cast a spell to dampen my ardour.
Catherine Am I unattractive, uninteresting?
Gawain Your husband is lucky to have such an attractive, interesting, *very* interesting wife.
Catherine He does not appreciate me.
Gawain He *trusts* me.
Catherine Hold me.
Gawain I cannot.
Catherine Just give me one kiss.
Gawain I must not.
Catherine Just one.
Gawain I promised.
Catherine Accept this lace girdle. (*She hands it to him*)
Gawain As a favour?
Catherine (*nodding*) And it will protect you from harm. It is magic—it will cost you one kiss.
Gawain Protect me?
Catherine No-one will harm you, if you carry it.
Gawain Just one kiss—no price at all to pay in any circumstances. And if the girdle protects me, it is worth a thousand kisses. (*He kisses her*)

They are disturbed by the return of the White Knight and Giles

Gawain hides the girdle

White Knight (*bellowing*) My blessed horse shed a shoe. No hunting for me today. (*He pauses*) How about you, Gawain?
Gawain No.
White Knight No little confessions?
Gawain No—I am a Knight of the Round Table!
White Knight (*to Catherine*) You must be losing your touch, dear. Many have been tempted by your beauty.
Catherine Gawain is an honourable knight, husband. And I am an honourable wife.
White Knight (*laughing*) So, Gawain, you did not enjoy a single kiss, accept a single favour.

Gawain (*hesitating*) I thank you for your hospitality, Sir Knight, but I must go in search of the Green Knight.

White Knight Pity... I am going to get a new horse and then I will be away hunting, probably be gone for two days.

Catherine Cannot you stay and protect me, Sir Gawain—the nights are cold and cruel.

Gawain (*can't take any more of this*) Please direct me to the Green Knight.

White Knight (*patting Gawain as he leads him off*) If that is your wish.

Gawain and the White Knight exit

Catherine (*miffed: after them*) Call that gallantry!
Giles (*aside*) I call that stupid.

Catherine and Giles exit

The scene changes to a bleak wasteland

Percivale enters alone, still without armour, and armed only with his spear

Percivale I have followed the Red Knight all over the kingdom, just missing him by turns. Coming across a knight he mortally wounded in Derbyshire; his hoof marks not washed away by the tidal flow along the Ribble's banks; the dung of his horse still steaming on a frosty morning in Cumbria. But I cannot catch him. Cannot retrieve the goblet. Cannot gain my knighthood. But *Sir* Percivale I will be. And do you know why I am so certain? It's not the fine clothes I wear, or my superior armoury. (*He holds up his spear*) It is this. (*He indicates the ring*) This ring, the name of whose owner I don't know. I will find her, but only when I can announce myself as *Sir* Percivale.

Percivale goes out

Queen Pellesse, wounded, is helped on by her daughter Elaine and Lancelot

Elaine My mother would have died, Sir Lancelot, if you had not come along.

Act I, Scene 4

Lancelot She still might, Lady Elaine. I don't think I can cure her. I have never seen such a dreadful wound. How did it happen, Queen Pellesse?
Pellesse The blow was struck by a knight called Sir Balyn.
Lancelot I will swear revenge.
Pellesse It is too late. Balyn lies dead, killed by his own brother Balan, who also perished in the fight. Victims both of ambition and the trickery of Morgana le Fay.
Lancelot Why did he attack you?
Pellesse He came upon my castle—Carbonek.
Lancelot The mysterious castle where the Holy Grail is said to lie.
Pellesse (*nodding*) He tried to take the Grail. When I tried to prevent it, he struck me with the Dolorous Spear.
Lancelot I have heard of it.
Elaine The very spear which pierced Christ's side as he hung on the cross; his blood still wet upon it five centuries later.
Pellesse Brought with the Holy Grail to this kingdom by Joseph of Arimathea.
Lancelot And how can you be healed?
Pellesse By only one knight, who must touch the wound with the Dolorous Spear.
Lancelot Which knight?
Pellesse You are a great and good knight, Lancelot, but it is one who will be the greatest of all knights. He is not yet born... But he is near to conception...
Lancelot What do you mean?
Pellesse I am tired. Good night.

She retires to the pavilion

Lancelot and Elaine share a moment

Lancelot She is lucky—to have such a daughter.
Elaine Every stab of pain her wound gives her, also jabs at me—in my heart. We are prisoners to it.
Lancelot (*putting his hand on her shoulder*) I wish I could take the hurt away.
Elaine Your touch is a balm—I've never known such gentle strength. (*She holds Lancelot*)
Lancelot Your touch, too, has soothing powers, massaging away the empty pit in my soul.

Elaine What troubles you?
Lancelot I cannot say. But I can stay ... tonight.

They touch fingertips

Is it possible that by touching we can reach down into each other, so the pain is numbed and the numbness by some miracle becomes joy?
Elaine It will be possible.

They go into the pavilion

Morgana appears. She is invisible to all others

Morgana Do I act, or will Lancelot's lust act for me? Perhaps I should send him a dreamy visitor to remind him of what he wants and what he's running from. Yes, I think I should. (*She beckons*)

Guinevere enters. She is almost in a trance. This is Lancelot's dream

Guinevere I am in Lancelot's dreams tonight. Just as he is in mine, at Camelot. Even now, as he lies with Lady Elaine, it is my hair he strokes, me he kisses, my warmth he feels. I take no pleasure in this. We are wracked, tracked and hounded by this sweet love that cannot be, but is. And now he wakes and turns and sees, not me, but poor Elaine, who will recoil at his horror when he sees her and not me.

Guinevere leaves

Morgana watches

Lancelot gives an anguished cry. He runs, wild-eyed from the pavilion. Elaine follows

Elaine What's the matter?
Lancelot I have betrayed you.
Elaine How, we have just made love.
Lancelot Don't say it.
Elaine It would be dishonest not to.
Lancelot Too much dishonesty, deceit, has passed here.

Act I, Scene 4   35

Elaine Are you married?

He shakes his head

   Betrothed?
Lancelot Cursed.
Elaine Because we made love?
Lancelot Because I love someone else. And that love is the curse. It leads me to think of her even when I try to put her out of my mind—which I don't wish to. It makes me disloyal to my greatest friend. (*Gently*) It has caused me to use you, sweet Elaine, who I would never hurt.
Elaine I think we could be happy.
Lancelot I wish we could. This curse has caused disloyalty, pain and deceit. It means I cannot ever be happy, or bring happiness to those I'm with. The only solution—half-solution—is to banish myself, so that I don't taint others. (*Ironically*) Who knows, I might find happiness in my solitary madness...

He leaves

Elaine (*forlorn*) I love you.

Elaine goes off

Change of scene—the evil red world of the Red Knight

   The Red Knight, in full armour with mace and shield, enters. Percivale arrives on the scene

Percivale Caught you, you red-clad rogue.

The Red Knight ignores him. Percivale chases

   Stop, you scarlet scallywag.

The Red Knight carries on

   Do you hear, you rouge ruffian? (*He challenges him with his spear*)

The Red Knight stops

Red Knight Did you speak to me, swineherd.
Percivale *Goat*herd.
Red Knight Terribly sorry.
Percivale I have come for the goblet you stole from King Arthur.
Red Knight You'll get more than you bargained for. If you were armed I would slay you now. (*He moves on*)
Percivale Don't turn your back on me. (*He throws a stone at the Red Knight and hits him*)

The Red Knight charges, knocks the spear from Percivale's hand, then toys with him

Red Knight (*enraged*) Why, you dolt, you peasant, you serf. If a fly troubles me, it will be squashed, swatted. (*He lashes madly with his mace*) I'll feed you to the swine.

Percivale dodges frantically

Ha—a spineless, ill-bred coward. He runs like a dog.

Percivale turns to face him

Percivale Hand over the goblet, you rusty oaf.
Red Knight (*charging*) No-one speaks to me like that.
Percivale Hand me the goblet.
Red Knight (*lunging*) I will hand you this. (*He lunges*) And this. (*He lunges*) And this. (*He lunges*) Now you breathe your last. (*He taunts with the goblet in hand*)

Percivale finds his spear

Percivale No, thief, it is you who vanishes like a red stain into the earth. (*He spears him*)

The Red Knight dies. Percivale raises the goblet

To a coward, murderer and thief who is no more. I think his armour and his shield will suit me well. I'll have to see if I can't wash away the disgrace and bring some credit to its crest.

Act I, Scene 5   37

Gonemans, a hermit, appears. Gonemans is Merlin in disguise and unrecognisable

Gonemans So young Percivale will become a knight. (*He calls to him*) What are you doing, young sir?
Percivale I am pledged to the Court of King Arthur, and I need the Red Knight's suit of armour.
Gonemans You need more than armour to be a knight. I am the hermit, Gonemans. Come with me and I will show you the ways of knighthood.
Percivale I will gladly accept your offer, Gonemans. But let us relieve this ruffian of his armour first.

Gonemans and Percivale carry off the Red Knight

SCENE 5

Castle Carbonek

The Wastelands are barren, drenched in gloom. In one area we see the Green Knight's banner

Gawain arrives

Gawain What a place to meet your end, Gawain. Who'd have thought all your hopes would end in this God-forsaken setting. Maybe it's fitting— there's no glory attached to this.

The Green Knight appears

Green Knight Ah, you've come to receive your treatment, Gawain.
Gawain Can I beg for mercy?
Green Knight You can, but I won't grant it. When you struck my head off you were confident you would not have to receive a similar blow. But what challenge would that have been? (*He motions Gawain to lean over a tree stump*)
Gawain Do your worst.
Green Knight A single blow on the neck, as I recall. (*He raises his axe*) Just a single blow.

As the Green Knight is about to let the axe fall, Gawain straightens up

Come, come, Sir Gawain. Surely you're not frightened.
Gawain I am sorry. (*He leans over the stump again*)
Green Knight It is a fearsome power, the power of life and death. I just let the axe fall, expend no energy, and a life is ended. All the hopes, dreams, possibilities ended.
Gawain Do it... Do it now. The life of fear I have lead this last year had no hopes, dreams, or possibilities—the shadow of your axe saw to that. Do it now.
Green Knight You kept your bargain—almost.
Gawain I kept it totally—I returned to you. Make your blow and make it quick. This awful moment has already lasted twelve months.
Green Knight Yes, yes. But your bargain with the White Knight.
Gawain What has that to do with you? Stop playing games—I'm not a fish on a line.
Green Knight Very well. One blow with my axe. (*He brings the axe very slowly down on Gawain and draws it lightly across his neck*) Honour is served. Stand, Sir Gawain.
Gawain (*puzzled*) Why have you not killed me?

The Green Knight transforms magically into the White Knight

White Knight You did not break my trust by succumbing to temptation. The scratch on your neck is for the girdle which you accepted from Lady Catherine out of fear. You believed it would protect you.
Gawain Is this a game?
White Knight A test.
Gawain Do not be too hard on your wife, Sir Knight.
White Knight She was a party to my plan. You have proved yourself, Gawain.

The White Knight leaves

Gawain exits

From a cave/tent, Percivale emerges now in his red armour. He practises with his sword

Gonemans, the hermit, appears

Gonemans You have learnt well, Percivale.
Percivale Thank you, Gonemans. I feel confident. Not just because I can handle a sword, target a lance, or ride as well as most. Confident because I believe in myself.
Gonemans "Knowing" the ways of knighthood won't make you a knight.
Percivale I will *live* the ways—not just act them or talk them. Live them.
Gonemans That ring you wear.
Percivale It belongs to the woman I love.
Gonemans It looks familiar. Who does it belong to?
Percivale I don't know her name.
Gonemans How can you love her?
Percivale She's the most beautiful woman I have ever seen.
Gonemans Beauty is only skin deep.
Percivale So my sister Dindrane keeps reminding me.
Gonemans Now I have a daughter who will shortly be returning here. She's a fine woman—kind, gentle, warm, humorous.
Percivale I'm sorry, old friend, but my heart is set on the owner of this ring.
Gonemans As you will.
Percivale Thank you. Thank you for everything. I would like to stay, to meet your daughter. But I must return to Camelot soon.

Gonemans returns to the tent/cave

Bors enters. He is looking for Lancelot

Bors Lancelot... Lancelot... (*He goes to Percivale*)

Gawain enters

They all greet each other

Gawain, Percivale. It looks as though you caught up with the scarlet brigand. It's good to see you've still got your head on, Gawain.
Gawain Why are you calling Lancelot? Where is he?
Bors I don't know. A messenger came; he had met Lancelot in the Wastelands, half out of his mind by all accounts, wandering blindly, talking of betrayal.

Gawain Lancelot wouldn't betray anyone. He couldn't find it in himself. He just wouldn't.
Lancelot (*out of view*) Wouldn't he!

Lancelot should emerge out of either rocks or earth. He is dishevelled, distracted

Bors Cousin, what has happened to you?
Lancelot I've been foolish, selfish, unchivalrous.
Bors How?
Lancelot What does it matter?

Elaine appears to Lancelot

The others freeze, or are bewildered by Lancelot's behaviour and do not see Elaine. She is pregnant

(*Falling to his knees*) Elaine, forgive me.
Elaine It really doesn't matter.
Lancelot It hurts me more when you say that. How could I have been so callous.
Elaine I have my own fate. My own destiny. It is tied up with my unborn child. Not with you.
Lancelot You are right to punish me.
Elaine I am not punishing you. It is your own self-pity which is doing that. You have your own destiny to meet, just as I have mine. At the end of it all we might not be as far apart as you think. Now I must leave.

Elaine exits

Bors goes to Lancelot

Bors It is good to see you. Now we can return to Camelot with our greatest knight.
Lancelot Ha—you do not know me.
Bors Listen—do you believe in the Oath of Chivalry?
Lancelot Of course. But I have broken it.
Bors Do you regret that?
Lancelot Of course. The regret has driven me mad.

Act I, Scene 5

Bors Do you repent?
Lancelot Of course.
Bors Then come back. Be a knight. Be a better knight.
Lancelot Could I?
Bors It's all you can do—you have to.

Lancelot nods

Mordred and Morgana appear, unseen to the others

Morgana So, these are the chosen knights of Camelot—a deranged philanderer, a love-sick goatherd, the aptly named Bors, and Gawain who takes cover in a woman's skirts rather than face his challenge.
Mordred And where is the old wretch Merlin? Dead, pushing up the daisies, I have heard.
Percivale I'll ask Gonemans what this place is. (*He calls*) Gonemans.

Merlin appears at the entrance to Gonemans' cave, discarding Gonemans' robe

Merlin! Where's Gonemans?
Merlin I am one and the same. It's tiring being a magic man all the time. People always expecting me to cure blisters and boils. So I take time off as a hermit every so often.
Bors Good to see you, Merlin.

They pat Merlin's back, shake his hand

Merlin Don't make such a fuss. You asked where we are, and if you stop knocking and shaking the wind out of me, I will tell you. This is Castle Carbonek.
Lancelot Where the Holy Grail is lodged.
Gawain Let us find it, take it back to King Arthur.
Morgana (*unseen by them*) Yes, take it, take it.
Merlin No! The one who is to touch the Grail is not yet born.
Bors Aren't we worthy?
Merlin You are all worthy—but not worthy enough.

They are disappointed

But you four above all are worthy enough to see the Grail.
Percivale Even me?
Merlin Yes, Percivale, I know better than anyone of your virtues. Soon Castle Carbonek will change its form and be transported away until the time is right for the chosen knights to seek it once more, in your greatest quest—the Quest for the Holy Grail. If anyone not of good heart should look on the Grail they will be blinded or even struck down dead.
Morgana Don't take any chances, Mordred.
Mordred It's not fair.

Morgana and Mordred cover their eyes

Morgana My time will come. Very soon, it will come.

Heavenly music plays

The four veiled Grail Maidens appear with a casket and a spear. They are Blanchfleur, Dindrane and First and Second Grail Maidens. We cannot see their faces

Mist rolls down obscuring them. The four knights and Merlin kneel and bow their heads

ACT II

Scene 1

The court at Camelot—the Round Table

There is a goblet on the table

Lancelot and Arthur fight with swords or maces

Watching are Bors and Gawain, who tend to support Lancelot; and Mordred and Kay who support Arthur. Percivale, Dindrane, Merlin, and, most of all, Guinevere are ambivalent in their support

We believe the battle is to the death. Mordred sidles up to Guinevere

Mordred (*slyly*) And who would you have win, your Highness? Your husband, the good King Arthur, or Sir Lancelot, your...
Guinevere Hush, Mordred, or you might find yourself on the sharp end of a pike.

Mordred laughs dismissively. Arthur knocks Lancelot's sword from his hand and points his at his neck. There is a tense silence

Arthur (*laughing*) Next time, Lancelot, I'll loan you Excalibur.

Lancelot turns away, brooding

Merlin (*to the audience*) Time has run on eighteen years since Bors, Gawain, Lancelot, and Percivale returned from Castle Carbonek, having seen the Holy Grail. When they returned, King Arthur, too, saw Percivale's virtues. (*He waves his arm*)
Arthur I will add another knight to your number. Percivale come to me.

Percivale, wearing the red armour, approaches

Kneel, Percivale. You recovered my goblet as you promised. You have proved that you are at least the equal to many high-born knights, (*pointed to Kay*) better than many.
Kay I always knew he would be a great knight.
Arthur (*dubbing Percivale*) Arise, Sir Percivale.

Merlin stands by the vacant covered siege

Merlin Great indeed. (*He removes the cover to reveal Sir Percivale's name*) Sir Percivale, you might occupy this siege as one of the Great Knights of Logres, along with Bors, Lancelot and Gawain.

Dindrane goes to stand with Percivale

(*To the audience*) *Sir* Percivale still wears the ring of the mysterious woman he has yet to meet again.

Merlin moves to Lancelot, who still broods

(*To the audience*) And Sir Lancelot, recovered, he thinks, from his time in the Wilderness, is growing impatient.
Arthur Our fight was good sport, Lancelot.
Lancelot Sport is all it is. Jousting, fencing. Just sport.

All look at Lancelot

Bors It's also good practise.
Lancelot Practise! What for? The next tournament?
Gawain The next quest, Lancelot.
Lancelot It seems the time between each adventure, each challenge, stretches.
Arthur That is because you have driven out most of the evil doers. And the Saxons daren't cross our borders any more.
Guinevere Aren't you content here, Lancelot?
Lancelot Perhaps I want what I can't have.
Arthur Perpetual adventure?

Lancelot and Guinevere exchange the slightest glance

Lancelot That must be it.

Act II, Scene 1

Gawain Merlin, you keep promising the greatest adventure of them all. At this rate we'll not be fighting with swords, we'll have to use crutches and walking sticks. We'll be old men.
Merlin There's nothing wrong with being an old man—apart from the groaning joints and lack of breath. I'm seven hundred and fifty nine—do I complain?
Mordred You never cease.
Merlin Well, some people, Mordred, give me cause to.
Arthur When will the quest for the Holy Grail commence? Many of our number are spread far and wide, seeking the mysterious Castle Carbonek, determined to bring the Holy Grail to Camelot.
Merlin Only one will hold it and he is not yet here—quite. The Siege Perilous is still vacant.
Kay Can this newcomer be so very, very good?
Merlin If he were not, he would die if he took his place in the Siege Perilous or die if he held the sacred Holy Grail. For over eighteen years, a boy without a father has been growing, growing strong. He has inherited his mother's gentleness.

A young knight dressed in white enters. He carries a shield with four stars on it. But he has no sword. It is Galahad. He heads for the Siege Perilous, then bows to Arthur

Many of the knights are affronted by this, none more so than Kay and Mordred

Mordred Pipsqueak—you should be cut down on the spot, entering unannounced.
Kay Merlin—where is the thunderbolt to cure this interloper of his impudence?
Mordred (*drawing his sword*) I will cure him.

Lancelot challenges Mordred

Arthur What is your name?
Galahad I am Galahad.
Arthur And you come here unarmed. Are you brave or a fool?
Galahad Let history decide, sire.
Merlin Who gave you your shield, Galahad?

Galahad The White Knight. It was brought to Logres from the Holy Land by Joseph of Arimathea.

Merlin removes the cover from the Siege Perilous. "Sir Galahad" is inscribed upon it. There is also a sword

Merlin History has decided. (*He hands the sword to Galahad*) This sword belongs in your scabbard. With it, Sir Balyn, who struck the Dolorous stroke, killed his brother. Galahad, by your good deeds, will you exorcise its evil.
Arthur I will make you a knight, Galahad.
Merlin There is one here whom I think is more appropriate. Who are your parents?
Galahad I know not my father——
Kay I knew it—he's a bastard.
Arthur (*angrily*) Hush, Kay—or that tongue of yours will never wag again.
Galahad —But my mother is Lady Elaine, daughter of Queen Pellesse. My father, I don't know his name, was one of the greatest knights.
Arthur Who should bestow knighthood on Galahad if it is not the King?
Merlin The boy's father.

Lancelot steps forward

Lancelot.

Lancelot nods

Many years ago, when you lay with Elaine, daughter of Queen Pellesse...

Guinevere lowers her head

Lancelot So not only evil flowed from that encounter.
Galahad Elaine is my mother.

Lancelot and Galahad embrace. Guinevere moves away distressed, but stays on stage

Lancelot You have washed away the years of madness and pain that I carried... Kneel, my son.

Act II, Scene 1

Galahad does so. Lancelot dubs him

Arise, Sir Galahad.

The five knights of the sieges stand in a row, Galahad in the centre. They raise their swords

The glory of the Grail will truly come to Camelot now.

The five knights go to leave

Arthur Discover the whereabouts of Castle Carbonek. Remember its form might have changed.
Merlin Remember also that others might want to hinder, subvert your quest for goodness.
Arthur May God go with you. Lancelot, a word.

Four siege knights leave

Lancelot goes to Arthur. Dindrane watches their exchange

I rely on you, Lancelot. You have proved your worth. Your boy might be good and brave, but I know that it is on you that the future of Logres will depend. Now say farewell to Guinevere—she would not forgive me if you left without bidding her adieu.

Lancelot pauses, looks at Guinevere

Go on, man. Nothing is so pressing that it can't wait one minute.
Lancelot If you wish it.
Arthur Now I must see Merlin. (*He goes to Merlin*)

Lancelot goes to Guinevere. Mordred watches them

(*Confidently*) Merlin, these are exciting times. Soon we will be secure. Having found the Grail, we will well and truly be God's chosen dynasty.
Merlin No matter what magic I enact, and what blessings are given from above—it is men, peoples, who ensure the goodness of the land we inhabit.

Arthur Don't play word games, Merlin. I, my court, will be God-given rulers. Anyway, no king could be surrounded by better people.

They continue talking

Lancelot What a day—a glorious day. I find my son. And who could expect to have such a fine son. Perfect.
Guinevere (*sadly*) A perfect day.
Lancelot I thought you, more than anyone, would share my joy.
Guinevere I don't share your boy.
Lancelot It was eighteen years ago. (*Bitterly*) I even imagined that poor desperate Elaine was you. It drove me mad.
Guinevere I imagined I was she.
Lancelot Don't be jealous.
Guinevere I am not jealous of her. I am jealous of the time we haven't spent together. Many would be jealous of the unswerving love that Arthur offers us both.
Lancelot I know.
Guinevere Take good care, Lancelot.
Lancelot I will soon return with the Grail for you.
Guinevere It shall be proclaimed that it is for the whole of Logres.
Lancelot Yes, of course.
Guinevere (*quieter*) But I know it shall be for me.

He kisses her hand, and leaves

Guinevere sees Dindrane watching

What is it, Dindrane?
Dindrane I pray for goodness to come to Camelot.
Guinevere So do we all.
Mordred (*aside*) Goodness will indeed come to Camelot—it will be called King Mordred.
Dindrane I must leave also.
Guinevere You?
Dindrane My destiny lies towards Carbonek.
Guinevere You can't leave... I will be so alone.
Dindrane Especially as *he's* gone?
Guinevere Don't make that sound like an accusation.

Act II, Scene 1

Dindrane It was supposed to sound like the truth.
Guinevere Don't despise me.
Dindrane I don't. (*She explains*) Perhaps it is because you're a queen—the public scrutiny becomes private scrutiny. The only way out of your obsession is to think not of yourself.
Guinevere You're saying I'm selfish.
Dindrane It is all right for monarchs to be selfish—or so it seems. For others it is necessary to think of the greater good.
Guinevere If I am selfish, then you are self-righteous.
Dindrane I am frightened of what lies ahead in the Wastelands and what lies in our hearts. (*She turns to go*)
Guinevere Dindrane.

Dindrane hesitates

Take care.
Dindrane (*smiling*) And you.
Kay (*calling to Arthur*) I too will go to the Wastelands. It seems it might be more exciting than here—this place is beginning to resemble a deserted monastery.
Arthur Good fortune, brother.

Kay leaves

Arthur, Merlin and Guinevere leave

Mordred is left. Morgana comes to him

Morgana Mordred.
Mordred Morgana, you have been conspicuous by your absence.
Morgana Biding my time.
Mordred (*angrily*) Waiting. Waiting. Comfortably growing old.
Morgana (*reacting*) Comfortably waiting! I have been grasping the blade of a two-edged sword these past eighteen years. My magic allied to Lancelot's lust created Galahad. How can that combination have produced this alleged *perfect* off-spring? Why have I had to wait till now, till this product of an unholy alliance, arrives?
Mordred So, the time has arrived.
Morgana I see the years have not dulled your ambition.

Mordred It has been carefully nurtured.

Morgana So I see. Well, the time has arrived. The destiny of Logres is dependent on finding the Grail. It is a flimsy society that puts all its hope on finding a cup.

Mordred You're a real romantic at heart, aren't you?

Morgana And you have the heart of a weasel and the brain of a toad ... which makes you perfect.

Mordred Thank you, madam.

Morgana (*nodding*) Let us go and see if we can't give Lancelot some of the adventures he craves for. One knight can lead us to the Grail. We will finish the others, one by one, on the way. Then destroy and desecrate the Grail, doing likewise to all the hopes that reside within it.

Scene 2

The Wasteland

It is dark, misty, frightening

Kay comes along. He is lost and frightened to a comic degree

Kay Oh Lord, a deserted monastery would have been preferable to this. Why didn't I stay at Camelot?

An owl hoots

I'm Sir Kay.

The owl hoots again

Are you deaf? I said I'm Sir Kay. (*He realizes*) It's an owl! I thought it said (*He imitates the owl*) "Who are you?" I'm going mad.

Gawain emerges from behind a tree and taps Kay on the shoulder

Kay jumps out of his skin

I submit. I surrender.

Act II, Scene 2

Gawain laughs

(*Turning*) Gawain, you great turnip-head.
Gawain You aren't afraid, are you, Kay?
Kay Afraid! Me! I only came to the Wasteland to look after you young knights.
Gawain That's very considerate of you.
Kay I know.
Gawain Because I have to admit I am afraid.
Kay (*brightening*) Are you? There's nothing to be afraid of.
Gawain (*suddenly*) Who is this?

Kay gets behind Gawain

We see a hooded figure carrying a candle—this is the Abbess of the Pathway

Abbess I am the Abbess of the Pathway.
Gawain We seek Castle Carbonek.
Abbess I know where you seek, what you seek, and why you seek it.
Kay Well, tell us where it is, then.
Abbess Sir Gawain, you may follow me. (*She beckons Gawain*)

Kay is unable to move

Kay I cannot move.
Gawain (*to the Abbess*) Sir Kay cannot follow.
Abbess Nor will he, he is not fit to see the Grail. A lifetime of bullying disqualifies him.
Kay No-one's perfect.
Abbess But you don't admit your faults. Or try to remedy them.
Gawain Go back to Camelot, Kay.
Kay If I wasn't stuck here, I'd teach that hooded candle holder a lesson. (*Aside*) As it is, I'll gladly return to Camelot.

Kay watches Gawain follow the Abbess onwards

Gawain and the Abbess exit

Mordred appears, startling Kay once more

Mordred! Does everyone have to jump out from behind trees and startle a fellow.

Mordred Have you found the way to Castle Carbonek?

Kay (*pointing*) That way.

Mordred Aren't you going on?

Kay (*lying*) Um no—a very important Abbess said as I was the bravest knight I should go back and protect Camelot. I don't think you'll see Carbonek, Mordred—because if it's a question of worthiness—and I'm not saying it is—you have no chance.

Mordred We shall see.

Kay leaves, back towards Camelot

Mordred is about to continue when he sees the Knight of the Forest with Dindrane tethered about his neck. The Knight wears a great horned helmet. Dindrane calls for help

Dindrane Help, Mordred. Help me.

Mordred I cannot be delayed in my quest just to save one useless maiden. Not so pious now, are you Dindrane? Not so choosy. It'll teach you not to be so holier-than-thou.

Bors enters the forest

Mordred moves quickly to hide

(*Aside*) The Knight of the Forest looks capable of dispensing with Sir Bors—leaving a siege for me.

Bors confronts the Knight

Bors Let her go, Knight of the Forest.

Knight of the Forest I will take her, and the pleasure of it will be all the greater if my hands are wet with your blood.

Mordred (*as a distressed knight, hiding*) Help me, Sir Bors.

Bors stops, torn between helping Dindrane, and the concealed Mordred

Dindrane Help, Sir Bors.

Mordred Help me, Bors—I am your brother, Lionel. They're torturing me.

Act II, Scene 2

Dindrane Please help me.

Bors is in a dilemma

Morgana appears to us

Morgana Ha. Sir Bors is split apart by his conscience just as surely as though he was cleaved by a sword. His beloved brother, or so he thinks, and Dindrane, pure and helpless. Who shall he choose?
Mordred Help me, brother.
Dindrane Help your brother, Bors. He is more worthy than I.

This determines Bors to help Dindrane

Bors Come, Knight of the Forest—what is your quest? To attack defenceless women?
Knight of the Forest To rule this forest. To exercise my power as I will. Fight.

Bors and the Knight of the Forest fight. The Knight of the Forest is armed with a great carved axe, to Bors's sword. Bors eventually wins

The Knight of the Forest exits, wounded

Dindrane Thank you, Sir Bors.
Bors Now, I must go to rescue my brother.
Dindrane I suspect that was Morgana's trickery; didn't your brother go towards Caerlon. I am sure he is not here.
Bors (*nodding*) My brother would not have put his safety above yours.
Dindrane You must go on to Carbonek.
Bors Come on, then.
Dindrane No—I must stay and guide the others.
Bors You will be in danger.
Dindrane Are only men permitted to undertake adventures? It is my destiny, my choice, as much as your task is yours. I will stay. But you must go, for time grows short and Carbonek will disappear once more.

They kiss

Bors Take care, Dindrane.

Bors leaves

Morgana talks to Mordred, unseen by Dindrane

Mordred Why do you not prevent the knights going to Carbonek? I now know the way.
Morgana You insolent fool, Mordred. It is not an easy matter to stop them.
Mordred So it seems.
Morgana A raven tells me the next knight to come this way will be the great Sir Galahad. Already coming this far he has defeated many who would stop him.
Mordred I hope you don't want me to fight him.
Morgana   Ha! Let us see how he copes with this;
                    Demons of the dark
                    Even now hark
                    Demons arise
                    Set fiery eyes
                    Upon the Knight
                    Clad in White.

Two grotesque demons carrying tridents appear. They scurry, chatter

Sir Galahad arrives

Galahad What is this I see?
Demons   Demons of the dark
                    Even now hark
                    Demons arise
                    Set fiery eyes
                    Upon the Knight
                    Clad in White.

The Demons lunge at Galahad

Galahad (*deftly avoiding them*) Demons of the dark indeed. Pleased to meet you. I am in need of some sword practice. (*With each blow*) Go back—devil's disciples—to the depths—of dank despair—you—are—no—match—for goodness.

Act II, Scene 2

He soon sends them scurrying off

Mordred What now, Morgana?
Morgana (*chanting*) Dragon of the Forest
With fire blessed
Dragon awake
All is at stake
Destroy the Knight
Clad in White.

The Dragon appears behind Galahad

Dindrane (*warning him*) Galahad!
Dragon I am the dragon
I am a thousand fears
Who's haunted your dreams
For a thousand years
I am the monster
Who speaks in a hundred voices
Who on your guilt
Feeds and rejoices
Fight me if you will.
Galahad (*fighting the Dragon*) Sulphurous fumes—acrid—living pyre—beast—incarnation of Satan's fire... (*He pauses*)
Dragon You are brave, boy.
Galahad I am Sir Galahad.
Dragon You are brave, Sir Galahad.
But you are like all men.
All who come to kill me.
Because I am more powerful.
It fills you with fear. The fear stifles your understanding,
so though you must try to kill me,
you won't succeed.
Galahad I am not afraid of you. But my understanding tells me you are here to kill me, so that I might not pass in my search for the Grail.
Dragon You are like any hunter.
You want a trophy, something to hang on your wall,

something that you think
will make people think well of you.
Galahad You do not understand me, Dragon. A hunting trophy is nothing compared to that which I seek.
Dragon I know you speak the truth, for I have the wisdom of a thousand years. You are truly good.
Galahad Will you block my way?
Dragon Why should I? I will return to the mountains of the Lakes, where still I might find peace.
Galahad I trust you will, Dragon.

The Dragon leaves or becomes inanimate

Galahad comes to Dindrane

Lady Dindrane.
Dindrane You are drawing near to Castle Carbonek, Sir Galahad.
Galahad Might I escort you out of this forest?
Dindrane No, I must point the way for your father Lancelot, and my brother Percivale.
Galahad Should I wait?
Dindrane You must go on before Morgana hatches more plots to thwart you.
Galahad Take care, brave woman.
Dindrane Hurry on.

Galahad proceeds

Mordred and Morgana again talk, unseen by Dindrane

Mordred Knights, demons, dragons—what else can you do to stop them?
Morgana *She* must be stopped.
Mordred Shall I kill her?
Morgana She would outwit you. Besides, I will do it myself—I'll ensure she dies slowly... (*Her face covered and feigning illness, she goes to Dindrane*)
Dindrane Lady, are you unwell? This is an accursed place. It is not safe.
Morgana It doesn't matter. I am dying.

Act II, Scene 2

Dindrane Is there anything I can do to help you?
Morgana I would not ask it.
Dindrane You must.
Morgana Only by allowing the blood of a pure maiden to run into mine can I be saved.
Dindrane Take some of mine.
Morgana I couldn't.
Dindrane You must. What value is it to me, if I must watch you die for the lack of it. (*She offers her wrist*)

Morgana instantly produces a knife and cuts Dindrane's wrist. Morgana sucks the blood. Then Morgana stands

Morgana I feel better already. Heady. Happy. Ecstatic. A real pick-me-up.
Dindrane I feel weak ... dizzy.
Morgana Farewell, Dindrane.
Dindrane Morgana? Morgana le Fay!

Morgana hears Percivale and Lancelot arriving. She laughs and disappears into the trees

Dindrane is near to collapse as the two knights arrive

Percivale Dear sister, what has happened?
Dindrane You must go on to Castle Carbonek—I fear it will soon transform and be transported away once more.
Lancelot We cannot leave you here.
Dindrane I am dying, tricked by Morgana le Fay.
Percivale There must be something we can do. You are part of me. Leave you, and I leave my soul.
Dindrane No, my soul will be in you. Find the Holy Grail. Do that, and I can rest in peace. You *must* do that. You must.

They stand

Go—or it is all for nothing.

Percivale kisses Dindrane, and he and Lancelot go on

Morgana Now they have lead us to the Grail, Mordred. Let us see if it cannot be ours.

Mordred and Morgana leave

Two hooded monks come and take Dindrane away

Scene 3

Castle Carbonek

The castle is clearly enchanted. Sweet music fills the air

On the steps lies Pellesse, still injured from the Dolorous Stroke. By her side stands Merlin. Arthur and Guinevere are lower down

The five siege knights enter

Mordred and Morgana can be seen hiding

Four veiled grail maidens enter with spear and casket—they are First and Second Grail Maidens, and Dindrane and Blanchfleur; but we do not know that yet

Merlin Welcome, good knights, to Carbonek... Queen Pellesse here has suffered for many years, guardian of the Holy Grail, smitten by a knight, who, for his own ends, tried to take the Grail.

First Grail Maiden (*lifting her veil*) What is this thing, this mere object, that men and women would die for, kill for, suffer for? What does the "Holy Grail" mean?

Second Grail Maiden (*lifting her veil*) It might be said to be a simple cup. But simple things can have great meanings and purpose, just as grand, elaborate designs might in the end be trivial.

First Grail Maiden This simple cup, the Grail, was used by Our Lord to administer the First Sacrament to his disciples at the Last Supper.

Second Grail Maiden The Dolorous Spear pierced his side as he hung on the cross.

First Grail Maiden Joseph of Arimathea brought them to this land soon afterwards and here they have lain for half a millennium.

Act II, Scene 3

Merlin So what is their meaning? Do they have a magical quality—or is the magic in the belief, the faith of those who follow? All of you will give it your own meaning. Your own self-belief will be the test of your strength.

Pellesse And whoever has the strength and is virtuous enough to take the Spear to cure my wound from the Dolorous Stroke. That same person will carry the Grail to heaven, and a shaft of sunlight will shine down on this kingdom.

Merlin These five are great knights, Queen Pellesse. But only one is great enough.

Morgana (*emerging*) One has deceived his King.

Lancelot It's a lie.

Morgana One left a maiden in the forest, putting the quest above her.

Bors She implored me.

Morgana One stole a ring, and his vanity would not let him consider Gonemans' daughter for fear she might be plain.

Percivale I still love the woman whose ring I exchanged.

Morgana One took a gift out of fear, a girdle to protect his life.

Gawain Is it wrong to fear death?

Arthur These are human traits. These weaknesses are the strength of being human.

Galahad I sense that I am the one who should take the Holy Grail—that I do not belong in this world. In my eyes that makes me imperfect.

Merlin You are chosen, Galahad.

Galahad I never make choices for myself. I do what is right. I am not half the man that my fellow knights are, for I don't have dilemmas.

Pellesse You are chosen.

Lancelot Go, my son.

The four siege knights bow to Galahad, who goes up the steps. He holds his sword as a cross. He takes the spear from one maiden and touches Queen Pellesse's leg

Pellesse (*standing*) My leg is healed, Sir Galahad. You are indeed the chosen one. Now take the Grail...

Galahad takes the Grail from the casket. All bow

Mordred hides, unable to look

Percivale lifts the veil from the third grail maiden—it is Lady Blanchfleur

Percivale You wear my ring. You are the sleeping lady I have thought of every day since I saw you.
Blanchfleur I am Lady Blanchfleur—daughter of Gonemans.

Percivale goes forward and they meet

Percivale So, but for my vanity I would have met you long ago.
Blanchfleur We have met now.

Galahad lifts the veil of the fourth maiden—it is Dindrane

Percivale Dindrane!
Dindrane I go with Galahad to a better place, for our task is completed. It wasn't all for nothing.

Dindrane and Galahad ascend the steps. A choir sings as a mist envelops them. And they are gone

Castle Carbonek is bathed in golden light

Pellesse Percivale and Lady Blanchfleur—you will be King and Queen of Carbonek.
Arthur See the devastation of the Dolorous Stroke vanishes; flowers grow, the land is verdant, and sweet bubbling water washes away Evil's contamination. Percivale—your kingdom will be a great ally and peaceful friend of Logres. Logres will enjoy everlasting peace——
Merlin Not everlasting peace, sire.
Arthur Are we to be invaded?
Merlin Not by enemies of a distant country. Enemies in the "heart" (*he touches his breast*) of Logres. Soon darkness will descend.
Guinevere Let not prophets of doom ruin this great day. We must celebrate joy and love.

All ascend the stairs to music. Only Morgana is left

Morgana I have been wrong, so so wrong.

Morgana leaves distressed

Act II, Scene 4

Mordred emerges

Mordred (*angrily, to himself*) Yes, she has been wrong ... like the rest of them. But in one final act—I, Mordred, will use their basest motives to rid Logres of King Arthur and his wretched knights. One final act, when evil will prevail, and *I* will be Lord of this Realm.

SCENE 4

The Lake

Arthur and Guinevere walk. Other knights stand by. Mordred stands alone

Guinevere All Merlin's talk of troubles in Logres has come to nothing. Since Sir Galahad found the Grail, peace has reigned. Our craftsmen have made ploughshares, not swords. Our horses draw ploughs, not carry knights in combat. We have built houses, not battlements.
Arthur Perhaps Merlin's prophecies were those of an old man facing death. Pessimism about his own future clouding everything he sees. I will go to him.
Guinevere I will stay here awhile, the peace of the lake reflects the peace which abides in Logres.

Arthur exits

Morgana, who has been hiding, attracts Mordred's attention

Morgana Sir Mordred...
Mordred So much for your grand plans. Ashamed to show your face after Carbonek.
Morgana I took sanctuary in a nunnery.
Mordred (*laughing*) Scheming, as ever.
Morgana The light from the Grail cast light on my life.
Mordred And gave you time to plot and plan?

Unnoticed in the background, Lancelot goes to Guinevere

Morgana To reflect.

Mordred So have I.
Morgana You're turning your back on blind ambition, on evil.
Mordred Turning my back on you, Morgana.
Morgana It does not matter, as long as you've changed your ways.
Mordred (*laughing*) My ambition is not blind—it is clear-sighted. I am turning my back on your hokum pokum, your jiggery pokery, your spectacular but sorry sorcery. (*He turns and indicates Lancelot and Guinevere*) Far more powerful forces than you can muster, Morgana, are working for me.
Morgana I beg you not to——
Mordred Go, before I have you seized. I could increase my standing further by capturing the witch Morgana le Fay.

Morgana leaves

(*Aside*) And I must take news to the King.

Mordred leaves

Lancelot and Guinevere talk

Guinevere I have always loved you, Lancelot.
Lancelot And I you, Guinevere.
Guinevere Over the years it has not waned.
Lancelot Unfulfilled desire does not. It lies inside heavier and heavier.
Guinevere At least we can be close at hand.
Lancelot I regret now there aren't any more great quests to take me away from Camelot.

Guinevere looks

So that my desire, my guilt, can't be twisted into vengeance against all who would stand in my way. I love you.

They kiss passionately

Arthur returns with Mordred, unseen by Guinevere and Lancelot

Mordred See, sire, they meet secretly—as they have for years. They

Act II, Scene 4

conspire—as they have for years. They humiliate you—as they have for years.
Arthur (*enraged*) Cease. (*He calls*) Seize Sir Lancelot.

Bors, Gawain, Kay, and Mordred run to the scene. Merlin comes and watches

Lancelot manages to escape

Guinevere is captured

Guinevere (*screaming*) Lancelot, do not desert me.
Arthur That's the real Lancelot. The coward, the conspirator. Will he even shed a tear when he sees and smells the smoke of your pyre. (*To the others*) She will be burnt at the stake—for treason and adultery.
Gawain Sire, hear her side.
Arthur I have seen enough. Heard how she called him for help, not begged me for mercy. She will burn in a hell that I will have to live with. The two I have truly loved have shown I was nothing to them. Burn her!

They lead her to the stake

Mordred (*enjoying this: to the audience*) Come warm yourselves at a royal bonfire.

Guinevere is tied to a stake. A bonfire built at her feet

Guinevere I have always loved you, Arthur, and been loyal. Even when it meant denying feelings I had no control over.
Arthur I have no control over my feelings now. Nothing matters any more. Torch her.

Drums build to a crescendo

Lancelot appears, with sword, rushing to Guinevere

Lancelot No. She is innocent.
Arthur Kill him. Kill him.
Bors Hear them. I don't beg. I insist.

Arthur You too will die for treason, Sir Bors.
Bors Listen to reason, sire.
Arthur The humiliation stops now.
Kay Gawain, help restore the honour of Logres.
Gawain Lancelot should be heard.
Merlin Gawain is right.
Arthur You knew of this Merlin; Lancelot has had his way for too long.

Arthur lunges at Lancelot, who strikes back defending himself

Gawain Lancelot, you have struck my King. My loyalty must be to him.

And so Kay, Arthur and Gawain fight Bors and Lancelot. Mordred hangs back. Lancelot kills Gawain

Kay Gawain is dead...

Morgana appears

Morgana Stop.

Bors is about to kill Arthur

Cease in the name of the Holy Grail.

They stop

Lancelot Is this your work, Morgana?
Morgana No, Lancelot. It is all of yours.
Bors We have slain a great knight and friend, Sir Gawain.
Mordred She is plotting, Arthur. Kill the traitors...
Merlin It is Mordred who has plotted.
Morgana I have come to repent, to beg mercy from my half-brother the King.

Arthur looks to Merlin

Merlin She is your step sister. I took you at birth to protect you. She was under a spell but now she has truly repented.

Act II, Scene 4

Mordred runs towards Morgana with his sword. Arthur goes to defend her. Arthur kills Mordred but Mordred manages to wound Arthur as he turns away. Arthur falls. They go to him

Arthur I am dying. Let there be no more quarrels.
Guinevere Forgive me, husband.
Arthur I forgive you, dear Guinevere. Return my sword to the lake.
Guinevere I cannot do it—it protects you.
Morgana Forgive me, brother.
Arthur I forgive you, sister. Return my sword to the lake.
Morgana I am not worthy to.
Lancelot Forgive me, friend.
Arthur I forgive you, friend. Return my sword to the lake.
Lancelot I could not do it.
Arthur Forgive me, all of you.

With a final effort, he throws the sword back into the lake. An arm rises to catch it, then it is gone. Arthur dies

Guinevere Oh no, he is dead. My beloved Arthur is dead.
Kay I failed him. All the time I was with him, for all my bravado and bluster, there was never a moment when I didn't guard him. Always a little brother needing watching. Now I have failed him. (*Ironically*) I think he liked me around because I made him look good.
Merlin He liked you around, Kay, because he loved you—and he knew you loved him.

Kay bows his head

Carry him to the barge: he and Excalibur will go to the realm of the Lady of the Lake.

Merlin watches them place Arthur on the barge

The knights leave

I too must take my leave. I will join the legions of knights who sleep. As King Arthur only sleeps. We will wait until we are needed.

Merlin goes

All Go in peace and love. The Knights of the Round Table will watch over you.

Arthur is born away on the mists of the lake. The company watch. Those dead, watch from above. Those alive, bow their heads

CURTAIN

FURNITURE AND PROPERTY LIST

ACT I

Scene 1

On stage: Stone with sword

Personal: **Hooded Figure:** baby
Igrayne: baby
Kay: scabbard without sword
Lancelot: sword
Bors: sword

Scene 2

Strike: Stone with sword

Off stage: Excalibur (**Stage Hand**)

Personal: **Pellinore:** lance, scabbard with sword
Arthur: sword
Percivale: roughly-hewn spear, ring
Lady Blanchfleur: ring

Scene 3

Set: 2 thrones
5 empty sieges (chairs), draped in silk (central siege slightly grander)
Round table. *On it:* goblet

Off stage: Breast plate (**Armourer**)
Gauntlets (**Ladies-in-Waiting**)
Helmet (**Ladies-in-Waiting**)
Lance (**Ladies-in-Waiting**)
Shield (**Ladies-in-Waiting**)

Personal:	**Percivale:** spear **Lancelot:** crown **Bors:** crown **Arthur:** sword **Sir Ector:** list of names, scroll **Red Knight:** sword **Gawain:** sword

Scene 4

Strike:	2 thrones 5 sieges Round table
Set:	Pavilion Goblet of wine Stone
Personal:	**Catherine:** lace girdle **Percivale:** spear, ring **Red Knight:** full armour with mace and shield, goblet

Scene 5

Strike:	Pavilion Goblet of wine Stone
Set:	**Green Knight's** banner Tree stump
Off stage:	Casket and spear (**Grail Maidens**)
Personal:	**Green Knight:** axe **Percivale:** sword

ACT II

Scene 1

On stage:	Round table. *On it:* goblet 5 sieges, 1 with cover and sword

Personal: **Lancelot:** sword
Arthur: sword
Galahad: shield with four stars
Mordred: sword
Gawain: sword
Bors: sword

Scene 2

Strike: Round table. *On it:* goblet
5 sieges, 1 with cover and sword

Set: Tree

Personal: **Abbess of the Pathway:** candle
Bors: sword
Knight of the Forest: great carved axe
Demons: tridents
Galahad: sword
Morgana: knife

Scene 3

Strike: Tree

Personal: **Grail Maidens:** spear and casket containing the grail
Galahad: sword

Scene 4

Set: Stake
Bonfire twigs
Barge

Personal: **Lancelot:** sword
Bors: sword
Arthur: sword
Kay: sword
Gawain: sword
Mordred: sword

LIGHTING PLOT

Property fittings required: nil
Various interior and exterior settings

ACT I, SCENE 1

To open: Overall general lighting

No cues

ACT I, SCENE 2

To open: Overall general lighting

Cue 1	**Lady of the Lake** leaves *Lighting becomes more magical*	(Page 15)

ACT I, SCENE 3

To open: Overall general lighting

No cues

ACT I, SCENE 4

To open: Overall general lighting

Cue 2	**Catherine** and **Giles** exit *Change to weak wasteland lighting*	(Page 32)
Cue 3	**Elaine** exits *Change to "evil" red lighting*	(Page 35)

ACT I, SCENE 5

To open: Gloomy wasteland lighting

No cues

ACT II, SCENE 1

To open: Overall general lighting

No cues

ACT II, SCENE 2

To open: Dark, frightening lighting

No cues

ACT II, SCENE 3

To open: Overall general lighting

Cue 4   **Dindrane** and **Galahad** exit   (Page 60)
         Golden light on Castle Carbonek

ACT II, SCENE 4

To open: Overall general lighting

No cues

EFFECTS PLOT

ACT I

Cue 1	**To open** *Mist and mournful chants of monks;* *woman's scream (can be done live)*	(Page 1)
Cue 2	**Merlin** appears *Mist changes colour*	(Page 1)
Cue 3	**Arthur** draws the sword from the stone *Music*	(Page 10)
Cue 4	To open Scene 2 *Mists and angels singing*	(Page 13)
Cue 5	**Arthur**: "I see no sword." *Haunting heavenly singing*	(Page 15)
Cue 6	**Percivale** and **Kay** square up *Roar of drums*	(Page 18)
Cue 7	**Morgana**: "Very soon, it will come." *Heavenly music*	(Page 42)
Cue 8	**Grail Maidens** appear *Mist rolls down*	(Page 42)

ACT II

Cue 9	To open Scene 2 *Mist*	(Page 50)
Cue 10	**Kay**: "Why didn't I stay at Camelot?" *Owl hoots*	(Page 50)

Cue 11	**Kay**: "I'm Sir Kay." *Owl hoots*	(Page 50)
Cue 12	To open Scene 3 *Sweet music*	(Page 58)
Cue 13	**Dindrane** and **Galahad** ascend the steps *Choir sings; mist*	(Page 60)
Cue 14	**All** ascend the stairs *Music*	(Page 60)
Cue 15	**Arthur**: "Torch her." *Drums build to a crescendo*	(Page 63)
Cue 16	**Arthur** is born away on the lake *Mists on the lake*	(Page 66)

www.ingramcontent.com/pod-product-compliance
Ingram Content Group UK Ltd.
Pitfield, Milton Keynes, MK11 3LW, UK
UKHW021845210426
5322IPUK00022B/484